THE GHOSTLY TALES OF VIRGINIA CITY

Published by Arcadia Children's Books
A Division of Arcadia Publishing
Charleston, SC
www.arcadiapublishing.com

First published 2022

Manufactured in the United States

ISBN 978-1-4671-9884-4

Library of Congress Control Number: 2022933035

Images used courtesy of Shutterstock.com; p.6 alexroch/Shutterstock.com; p. 74 Purplexsu/Shutterstock.com; p. 94 Capture 11 Photography/Shutterstock.com; p. 100 Arne Beruldsen/Shutterstock.com.

Adapted from *Haunted Virginia City* by Janice Oberding

arcadia
CHILDREN'S BOOKS

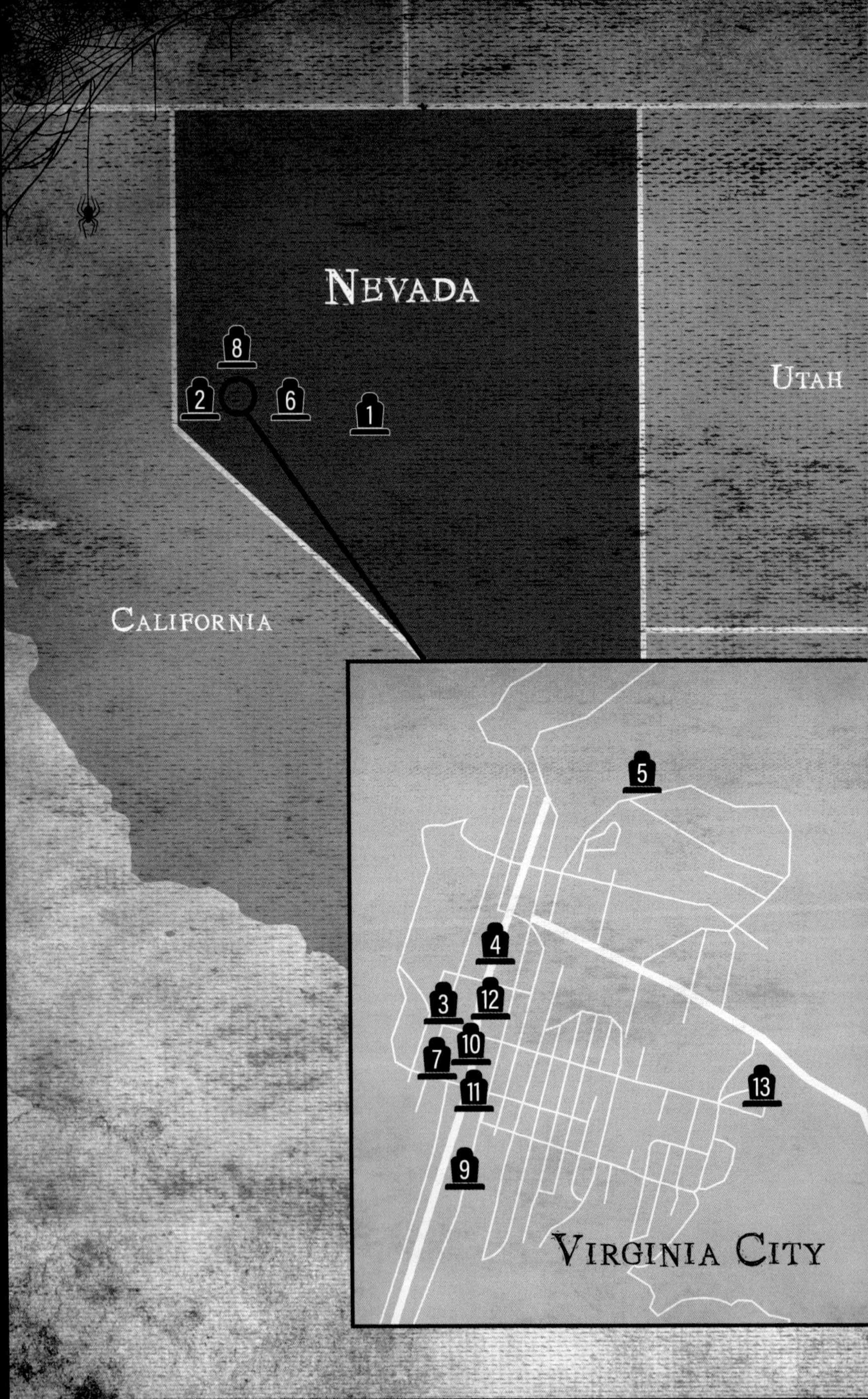
Nevada
Utah
California
Virginia City
1
2
3
4
5
6
7
8
9
10
11
12
13

Table of Contents & Map Key

WELCOME TO
VIRGINIA CITY
Please Drive Safely!

Introduction

Do ghosts really exist? Are they fact or fiction? It's a hard question to answer. If the answer is yes, why don't we all see them? Why is it so hard to prove? If they don't exist, how do we explain the things that some people see, like glowing orbs (floating balls of light) or translucent forms? How do we explain doors that close on their own, loud bangs in empty spaces, and strange scents? And what do we say to those who claim to have talked to ghosts? For the residents of Virginia City, Nevada, contact with ghosts is so frequent that it's hard to deny they truly exist.

There is a reason that Virginia City is popular with ghost hunters. The history of the city is completely tangled up with the spirits who still live there. Each time we tell one of the ghostly tales, we are also reliving the great silver rush and the miners who came to seek their fortune.

The biggest discovery of silver was called the Comstock Lode. When miners came to work, small cities popped up around them. Those men digging in the hills needed places to live, food to eat, and entertainment. Gradually, as they married and settled down, the towns needed schools, government, and all sorts of businesses.

Just about every building in the area, which came to be known just as "the Comstock," has a ghostly resident living there. For over a hundred years, celebrities have come to meet the ghosts. Television shows have been filmed in town. But even before TV and film, Mark Twain himself came to the Comstock to take a look around.

Let's look at the history of Virginia City and hear stories about the ghosts that live there now. In the end, it will be up to you to decide: fact or fiction? Do ghosts really exist or are they merely make-believe?

Turn the page and find out more . . .

Abandoned mine, Virginia City, Nevada

CHAPTER 1

The Beginning

The California Gold Rush began in 1848. Thousands of men headed west to find their fortune. Hosea and Ethan Allan Grosh left Pennsylvania in 1849 to join a wave of miners seeking riches. They tried their best, and even stayed long after others had given up, but their dreams didn't come true. They began to search for the next big opportunity.

In 1850, the United States Congress created the Utah Territory. Today, a lot of that land is currently part of Nevada, but at the time, it was uncharted, unknown to miners, and held great mystery. By 1852, rumors of another big gold discovery put people on the move. Dreams that had faded in California, were now refreshed and the Grosh Brothers joined the journey to the Utah Territory. This was the fresh start they'd been looking for.

When they arrived, the brothers immediately noticed that the area was not at all like California. This land was barren and dusty. In California, the miners searched for gold in streams and rivers. Here, miners had to cut through rock and hard ground with the hope of finding a small vein of gold.

This movement from California to the area that would soon be called Virginia City was called the Rush to Washoe. Washoe was the county named after the Native Americans who lived there.

While chopping away at the earth, hoping to find gold, these brothers noticed that the other miners were tossing aside a blue-colored ore. Having the experience of the California Gold Rush, they wondered if what they were looking at weren't worthless rocks. Could it be silver?

They decided not to tell anyone until they were certain. Every evening, while the other miners went out drinking and telling stories, the Grosh brothers studied. They read books on the science of metals, called metallurgy, and analyzed their ore samples. By 1856, they were certain that the stuff other miners tossed carelessly aside was truly valuable.

While they knew what they'd found, they needed official confirmation. It cost money to get a professional to confirm

the rocks were silver, and they didn't have any money. The men gathered up the samples and went back to California for the winter. There, they prospected for quartz and saved every penny they made.

A few months later, they still didn't have enough money to pay for the confirmation, but they didn't want to stay away any longer. The brothers decided to go back to Washoe and mine the silver veins that crossed Mount Davidson.

After they arrived, they had no doubt that this was the big one! The brothers began to dream. They were going to be very, very rich. Things were looking good until the bad luck began.

While out mining one hot morning, Hosea raised his pickaxe high and swung it hard toward the silver vein. He missed the vein and hit his foot instead. He cleaned the wound as best as he could, but those were the days before antibiotics and the wound became infected. Two weeks after the incident, Hosea died.

Ethan Allen was devastated. He missed his brother terribly. And yet, he pressed forward, living the dream for both of them. Ethan Allan refused to quit. He now had enough money to pay the professional to take a look at their silver ore. He packed up to go to California where the professional was living. While he was gone, Ethan Allan asked his friend, Henry Comstock, to watch his possessions, the cabin, and safeguard the silver vein for him.

A little trivia: Do you recall what the WHOLE area around Virginia City is called?

Hint: It's NOT called The Grosh . . .

Ethan Allen asked his buddy R.M. Bucke to go with him. They soon realized they should never have left so close to winter. The trip was difficult, and they ran into terrible snowstorms.

They were trapped in the Sierra Nevada Mountains. The matches they'd brought were all wet so they couldn't make a fire to warm up. When they ran out of food and supplies, the men had to eat their mule. But still, Ethan Allan was not giving up. He had to survive and get rich—for his brother! The men trudged on in knee-deep snow. Finally, they were rescued. They had to go to the hospital to recover. One of Bucke's legs was so badly frostbitten, it had to be amputated.

Ethan Allan had frostbite too. He also needed one of his legs removed, but he was stubborn. He refused the surgery and died. It had only been three months since his brother Hosea's death.

Both Grosh brothers were gone now, so what happened to the massive silver vein they'd discovered? Do you remember who Ethan Allan asked to watch over his home, supplies, and the area he mined?

Henry Comstock took it all. He used the Grosh brothers' maps and tools to claim the area as his own. Within the year, he discovered a large silver vein on the land. The Ophir Mine was built and the money began to flow. People from around the world came to the area to search for silver. The Rush to Washoe was booming.

Many historians consider Henry Comstock to have been lazy. Really, what did he do? He took advantage of the Grosh brothers' deaths to become very wealthy. The richest silver lode in the world was named the Comstock. Virginia City grew because of his Ophir Mine.

And yet, Henry Comstock met a similar fate to the Grosh brothers. For a moment, he was rich and famous—and then bad luck took it all.

Henry Comstock sold his share of the

mining claim for ten thousand dollars. He didn't know that it would eventually have been worth millions. Because he sold his own property, and spent more money than he had, it wasn't long before Henry Comstock was broke. He moved to Montana. In 1870, he was living with friends when he suddenly died.

Ghosts don't have to haunt where they were buried. They don't even have to stay in the place where they died. Henry Comstock died in Montana, but his ghost haunts Virginia City.

From the moment of his death, strange lights were seen in the Ophir Mine. Miners heard the echo of someone using a pickaxe to dig, in a closed off area far below the ground. One brave man, a young Irish miner, decided to find out what was going on. He went down into the mine in an elevator cage, following the sound. The noise got louder and louder. The man raised his lantern to look around.

Imagine his surprise when the ghost of Henry Comstock appeared, shouting, "I'm Henry Comstock, and this is my mine!"

"I know," the miner agreed as calmly as he could manage. He told the ghost he was leaving.

"Don't ever come back!" Henry Comstock warned.

The man didn't dare. One ghostly sighting was enough.

Throughout the years, other miners, guests, and visitors have reported seeing Henry Comstock at the mine. He's not always underground, but he's always there.

As for the Grosh brothers, their ghosts seem to have moved away from Virginia City. Maybe they were too upset to ever return. Or perhaps, they finally found their ghostly riches somewhere else.

CHAPTER

2

Old Virginny

So just how did Virginia City get its name? According to legend, it was from a man named James Finney, who was also known as Old Virginny. Whether the town's name came from his nickname, or the fact that he was originally from Virginia, no one knows for sure. But what we do know is that, just like the Grosh brothers and Henry Comstock, James Finney was an unlucky man. When he was about forty-four years old, James's horse threw him to the ground. He died shortly after. Perhaps Virginia City and the Comstock Lode are cursed . . .

Sandy and Eilley Bowers were unfortunate souls who also fell to the fate of this Comstock Curse.

In the nineteenth century, very few people got divorced. If a marriage wasn't working, usually both people stayed together, for better or worse. But not Alison "Eilley" Orrum. She was originally married to a man named Alexander Cowan.

When Alexander wanted to leave Nevada and move to Salt Lake City, he assumed Eilley would go along. She wasn't sure she wanted to go. Eilley was very spiritual and consulted her crystal ball. The "peep stone," as she called it, told her she'd be all right without her husband.

Eilley decided to stay in Nevada, but moved from the ranching settlement, where she and Alexander had lived, into Virginia City.

As more and more prospectors came to Virginia City, dreaming of riches, Eilley opened a boarding house. She made some money from that business, but she also bought and sold mining claims.

The peep stone told Eilley that she'd find another husband. Soon thereafter, she met Lemuel "Sandy" Bowers. While he was staying at the boardinghouse, the two of them fell in love. Eilley loved Sandy so much that when he hit hard times, before they were married, and couldn't pay his rent at the house, she agreed to take a small portion of his mining claim in exchange for free living. And then . . . Sandy struck it rich.

The Bowers were the first millionaires in

Virginia City. They moved to the finest home in the state. They spared no expense either inside or out. They even had ivy planted in the garden that they imported from Buckingham Palace in London! The house was built outside of the city limits in Washoe Valley. Such a fine house needed fine furnishings. They planned to buy the best carpets, artwork, antiques, and fabrics. Because they couldn't get what they wanted in Nevada, Eilley and Sandy decided to go to Europe.

Eilley was known as the "Queen of the Comstock" and the queen wanted a celebration fit for her new status. Right before their trip, the Bowers threw a massive party. They rented space in the International Hotel and invited the whole town. Cost didn't matter. The Bowers wanted their guests to have an incredible time. There was food, drink, and entertainment. Expensive champagne flowed like water. It was an unforgettable event.

It is said that while in Europe, Eilley wanted to meet Queen Victoria, imagining that the two queens should be friends. She had a special lavender dress made for the occasion. The Queen of England was not impressed enough to meet Eilley, after all the woman was a miner's wife! Eilley was so angry that when she got home, she had the gardeners remove all the British ivy plants from around the home.

Sandy died a few years later. It was quickly revealed that he'd either spent, or given away, all their money. He was known to have been a truly generous person, but left nothing for Eilley. She was broke. Eilley did what she knew best to survive. She began telling fortunes. The peep stone had given her answers when she needed them. Now she would use the stone to help others, and earn the money she needed.

If you are in Virginia City, be sure to visit the Bowers Mansion. The couple loved a good

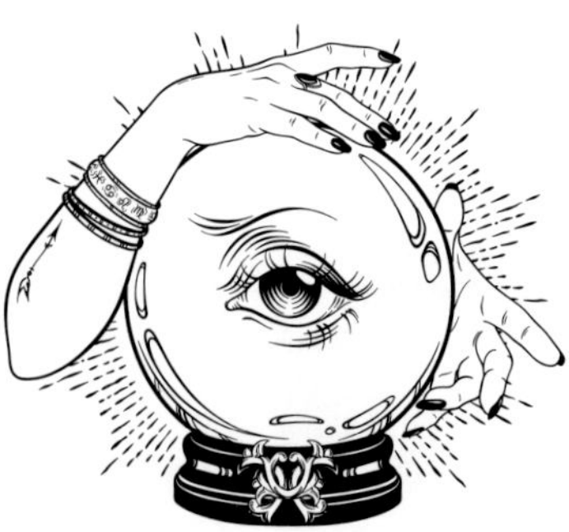

party in their life, and it's said that the party continues, now, even after they are gone. When the house is empty, and no one is on the street, there is always the faint sound of laughter, music, and the happy clink of champagne glasses.

Do you like a ghostly party? Be sure to wear your dancing shoes!

CHAPTER 3

The International Hotel

While you are at the International Hotel, don't forget to look for the other ghosts who haunt the halls.

When the hotel was built in 1860, it was a one-story wooden structure. Just two years later, more rooms were needed for all the visitors and miners coming to Virginia City. Two more floors were added. At the time, the builders proclaimed that the hotel was fireproof.

Maybe they shouldn't have bragged? Or perhaps, they should have been concerned about the curse that seemed to blanket those early days in Comstock.

On October 26, 1875, a fire swept through Virginia City, destroying a thousand buildings. Shops, restaurants, and homes all burned to the ground. And so did the International Hotel. A new building, built on the same spot, was even more grand than the original. Now, the hotel was six stories tall. The hotel covered an entire city block, from C to B Streets, which made it the largest building around.

As a stopping place on the way to San Francisco, the International Hotel had many famous guests. When President Rutherford B. Hayes came to town in 1880, he stayed there. John Mackay, a Comstock millionaire, had a permanent room at the hotel. New York senator Frank C. Platt enjoyed the hotel.

Other presidents such as Ulysses S. Grant and Benjamin Harrison made stops there too.

The hotel seemed like it had weathered the worst and everything was rosy after that first fire. Then, in December 1914, the hotel had a second blaze. This time, the fire destroyed the building in a few hours. Most of the building had to be rebuilt, that was, except for one curious room. A room on the B side of the street, called the Mystery Room, survived the blaze.

The fire hadn't touched it. The Mystery Room was left intact.

After the fire, there were a lot of questions as to why that one room didn't burn. Some people thought that the ghost of Jimmy Cummings was in there. Jimmy was a mail clerk for the railroad. But there was a secret. Jimmy wasn't really delivering mail, instead, he was going through it and stealing valuables. He knew the police were investigating him when he checked into the International Hotel.

Although Jimmy died in March 1900, years before the fire at the hotel, perhaps it was his spirit that safeguarded the Mystery Room. Could it be that he was hiding out in the room, in hopes of protecting himself from being arrested?

Bill Smith was another ghost who could have been hanging around. Bill was killed in the hotel saloon when Arthur Hefferner's pistol accidentally went off. The bullet hit Bill, who died instantly. Maybe he just didn't want to check out of the hotel—ever!

The ghosts of these men might have been protecting the Mystery Room They both had reasons to stay around after their death. Besides, the International Hotel was the finest place in town, and if you were looking for a place to haunt—wouldn't you want the very best?

After the fire in 1914, it was determined that the hotel wasn't worth saving. It was too expensive to rebuild. As the crew broke down the last bits of the structure, they were told to be on the lookout for a body. A jeweler named Paul Pinet was never found after the blaze. No one knew what happened to him.

Oddly, the demolition crew did, in fact, find a body, but it was never determined if it was Paul or someone else. Could Paul's spirit have settled into the Mystery Room after he died in another part of the hotel?

In 1933, the last bits of the International Hotel were removed. Along with those final charred pieces, the ghosts were pushed out, but where did they go next? There are certainly plenty of other places for ghosts to take up residence in Virginia City . . .

Samuel Clemens, aka Mark Twain

CHAPTER 4

The Writer's Return

Samuel Clemens was a famous writer. You might know him by the pseudonym, or pen name, he used: Mark Twain. When Samuel was just starting out as a writer and journalist, he traveled with his brother to Virginia City. Samuel worked at the *Territorial Enterprise*, a local newspaper. There, he became interested in stories about people, their success and failures. He honed his craft and wrote articles.

All this would eventually lead him to write the book *Roughing It*, which was about his time in Virginia City.

After he left town and moved away, Samuel came back a few times to give lectures, never forgetting the people and place he loved.

There are those who believe that Samuel Clemens/Mark Twain enjoyed Virginia City so much that he came back one more time—after his death. And has never left since.

Can ghosts appear in any form they want? It's an interesting question. Would an old man want to return as a young ghost? A young woman as a child? Can the ghost decide what clothing they want to wear or if they would prefer to just be an orb, a glowing ball of colored light?

What do you think?

For those who claim to see Mark Twain hanging around town, they identify him as a young man, full of life as he was at the beginning of his writing career. Perhaps, this is because Twain never visited the city when he was old. Or maybe this is his favorite form of himself?

There was a man who lived a short distance from C Street in the heart of town. He didn't like to drive so he walked everywhere. One night, he was out late. The man said goodnight to the bartender where he had been enjoying a drink and began the journey home. Along the way, he ran into someone dressed up like Mark Twain. Twain was known to have bushy, wavy hair and a thick mustache. He wore a long black jacket and thin bow tie. He smoked a pipe. The man was amazed. This Mark Twain costume was very accurate! He figured he was meeting someone in costume, maybe returning from a masquerade party.

The man complimented the old-fashioned costume. "Nice getup. Where ya goin'?" the man asked.

The stranger stared at him for a few seconds, then disappeared.

The man looked around, desperate to explain what he'd seen. But in the end, the answer was clear. He'd met the ghost of Mark Twain.

The man instantly decided he'd never stay out so late again!

CHAPTER 5

The Most Famous Ghost in Town

For years, the name Julia Bulette has been used on shops and restaurants in Virginia City. But who was she? No one really knows.

She wasn't wealthy. She wasn't famous. She wasn't popular.

Julia Bulette was a murder victim.

On January 20, 1867, she was found dead in her own bed. The news of Julia's death spread quickly through town. She knew a lot of people and everyone wanted the killer found. They demanded justice for Julia.

After the funeral service, her body was taken to a small area cemetery called Flowery Hill. But there are those that say she wasn't really buried at Flowery Hill. It's long been rumored that her coffin was filled with sand and her body stolen.

An undertaker, the man tasked to get the body ready for burial, was madly in love with Julia. Popular belief is that he was the one that filled the coffin with sand and buried her in his basement instead. He wanted them to be together forever.

What did Julia look like? It's known that she was an honorary member of the Virginia City Engine Company No. 1. There is a photo of a woman with a fire hat that some people think is Julia. It could be her, but many people believe the picture is of a fireman's wife from around the same time.

However, there is another photo, hanging in the Bucket of Blood saloon, that some say is Julia. But is it really? She doesn't seem to be the same as the woman with the fire hat, so who is she? Which photo is Julia? Maybe it's one or the other . . . or neither of them . . . We will never know.

Julia was last seen on January 19th, when she was turned away from Pipers Opera House for refusing to sit in an area assigned to lower-class women. We can imagine she was upset about this. The next thing anyone knew was that her friend Gertrude came to meet Julia for breakfast and found her body.

The police were called. They noticed that several items of Julia's clothing were missing. Some jewelry was gone too. The police said the murder was a robbery that had gone wrong.

No one really knows the circumstances of Julia's death. And maybe someone will be brave enough to ask her ghost. Because it's believed that Julia's spirit haunts the town.

A woman and child have been seen at Flowery Hill at the same spot where Julia was said to have been buried. It's possible that the woman might be Julia. But who is the child? As far as anyone knows, Julia never had kids.

Many ghost hunters think the woman at the cemetery cannot be Julia because it seems most likely that if the undertaker's story is true, her spirit would stay closer to the undertaker's apartment basement.

Early one morning, a woman who works close to that apartment building said that she was cleaning the countertops in a nearby shop. She was halfway through the job when she saw a woman standing in the corner. The shop wasn't open yet.

"Can I help you find anything?" the clerk asked the woman.

Suddenly, the summer air turned bitter cold. The woman in the corner slowly vanished. The clerk was certain this was Julia.

There is so little known about Julia Bulette. Julia wasn't famous in her life, but now, she's Virginia City's most popular ghost. And many people claim to have seen her spirit wandering around town.

Read on for the next part of this story.

There was a man arrested for Julia's murder . . .

CHAPTER 6

Did He Do It?

John Millian, a Frenchman, was arrested for the murder of Julia Bulette. But did John do it? Or not? Only his ghost knows the truth.

In 1868, John Millian was caught trying to sell stolen items—including several of Julia's things. Remember when the police said Julia's murder was a robbery gone wrong? Well, John had her coats and her jewelry. He claimed he was innocent. He said he was the lookout person for the actual robbers. He said he was watching the street to make sure they got away. John told the police that the robbers gave him some of the things they'd stolen. The court didn't believe John and he was declared guilty.

John was an attractive young Frenchman. When some young women in town heard he was going to be hanged for the crime, they baked him sweets and sent them to the jail.

On May 31, 1868, John was hanged for the killing of Julia Bulette.

Coincidentally, Mark Twain was in the crowd that day. Twain wrote about the hanging in the *Chicago Republican*. He wrote that John was such a bad man that many people wanted to see him hanged. Five thousand people came that day to witness John Millian's death.

Even till the last minute, John Millian said he was innocent. Just before he died, he spoke to the crowd in French. He told them he did not believe that he should be hanged for a crime he didn't commit.

More than one hundred years later, it's still not known if John was truly guilty or not. Many people believe that ghosts will appear because of injustice or unfinished business. Perhaps John Millian haunts Virginia City because he is still trying to convince people of his innocence.

If you are brave enough to seek out John and Julia, ask them what really happened on that tragic night in January 1867.

CHAPTER 7

Big Jack's Treasure

If you had a buried treasure, and then you died, would you haunt the area and scare people away? That's what Jack Davis decided to do. His treasure is hidden and he wants to keep it that way!

In the late 1800s, Jack Davis was a stagecoach robber. And he was good at it. "Big Jack" started out as a miner, but when he didn't find his fortune, he found another way to make money. He and his gang would rob coaches, wagons, and trains coming into western Nevada. They'd melt down the stolen gold and resell it, pretending that they'd found it themselves.

In 1870, Big Jack and his gang boarded a train somewhere between Verde and Reno, Nevada and then waited patiently. When the train crossed a barren area, with very few people aboard, they pounced. The train's engineer didn't have a choice. He stopped and let the men escape with $40,000 worth of gold and silver.

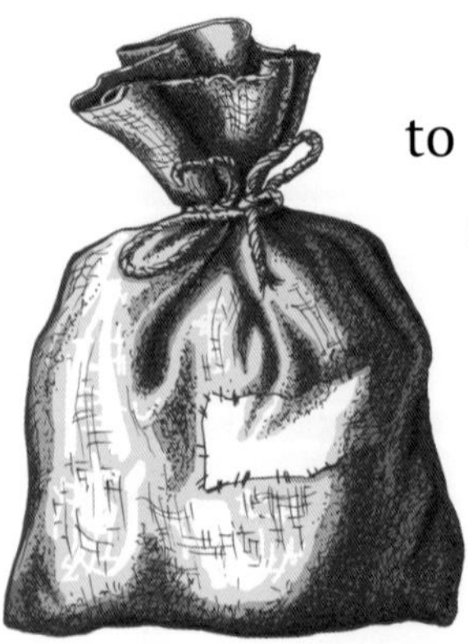

One of the robbers decided to brag about their luck. He was spending the stolen money and buying nice things. When the police asked him where he got the cash, the burglar confessed. All five men who had been involved in the robbery were arrested.

Big Jack was sent to prison. He was supposed to be there ten years, but after just one behind bars, there was a break-out. Twenty-nine prisoners escaped—but Jack Davis wasn't one of them. He stayed behind and told the police everything he knew about the break-out! Because he had been helpful to the police, Jack was set free in 1875.

Jack could have changed his life, but he chose to go right back to robbing stagecoaches. He was careful about which ones he chose, thinking he could get away with smaller, less risky jobs. Of course, robbing people is never a safe way to make a living. Big Jack was killed in a shootout in 1877. He died without telling anyone where he'd been hiding his loot.

It was known that he'd been stashing everything he'd stolen somewhere in Six Mile

Canyon near town, but the exact location still remains a mystery today. Treasure hunters have long wanted to find the riches that Jack left behind, but only his ghost knows the spot.

Many of these treasure hunters have met the wrath of an angry white phantom. The ghost screeches, in an ear-splitting shriek, at anyone who apparently gets too close to the treasure. The spirit of Big Jack Davis has been lingering for over a hundred years in Six Mile Canyon scaring off anyone who comes looking for his loot.

If you think you can get rich by stealing Jack's treasure, good luck! Big Jack doesn't want you, or anyone else, to have it.

CHAPTER 8

The Ghost Camel

The ghost of Jack Davis isn't the only spirit haunting Six Mile Canyon. Believe it or not, there is a ghost camel that lives there too.

But, the mystery question is: does it have one hump or two? No one has ever gotten close enough to find out.

If the camel has one hump, it might be one of the dromedary (one hump) camels that the U.S. Army imported to help haul materials to

Virginia City. If it has two, it's probably one of the Bactrian camels (two humps) that were brought to Nevada during the late 1800s. Either kind of camel could carry a lot of weight and can go without food or water for weeks.

And yet, there were a lot of problems with Virginia City's camels.

Camels were suited to life in a sandy desert, not to Nevada's rugged and rocky landscape. Also, the Comstock miners didn't like the camels. They thought they were ugly and unfriendly. The camels scared the horses. And yet, at the time, there were so many camels around that Virginia City had to ban them from wandering around the street during the day.

By 1875, the Nevada legislature decided to be more specific. They totally banned camels from all public roads. The camels were becoming a nuisance. Camel owners started to realize they had to do something. The camels were causing trouble.

It wasn't easy to get rid of a camel. Some owners weren't very nice and they simply set the camels free in the desert. Most of those camels died right away, but a few others survived and wandered aimlessly throughout the hills.

Witnesses say that after all this time, there is just one ghostly camel that remains. It follows a path through the canyons and then climbs over the top of Mount Davidson. On certain nights, when the moon is full, the camel stands in the light. On the ghostly beast's back there is a grinning skeleton!

Who is the rider? Is it one of the miners? Or a camel owner who didn't want to leave their camel alone for eternity?

It's a mystery, but if you visit Six Mile Canyon, on a clear night, when the moon is full—BEWARE!

CHAPTER 9

The Statue in the Basement

Professional ghost hunters like to visit Virginia City because there are so many ghosts. A few years ago, a crew chose to set up their cameras in the Mark Twain Book Store because it was commonly known that the basement was haunted.

The now-closed store was in the old Colonel Morris Pinschower Building, which was built in 1862. Over a hundred years, the building had been a Joseph Frederick Hardware shop, a bank, a livery stable, a garage, and a car dealership. So there was a lot of history, and potentially a lot of ghosts hanging around.

There was a statue in the corner of the basement that the ghost hunters wanted to check out. Tommyknockers, according to the Cornish folklore of England, are mythical elves that followed men into the mines. It's said that the Tommyknockers would warn miners, with loud knocking sounds, if a mine was going to cave in. That was when they were being good. They also were known to hide tools and switch lunch pails to tease the miners.

The statue in the basement of the Pinschower Building was of a Tommyknocker elf with a mischievous look carved into his wooden face. For a while, people had reported that the eyes on the statue would follow them, as if the elf was alive.

The ghost hunters were going to find out!

They turned off all the overhead lights. The only glow was from their cameras and some equipment they were using to track ghostly presences. The basement was very, very dark.

When the Tommyknocker's eyes were illuminated by the camera crew, the eyes didn't move. Something else did though!

One ghost hunter said there was a carriage and a small child hovering nearby. They also felt the presence of horses, which made sense because the building had once been stables.

Hunters with digital recording devices called out into the dark. They asked if there was a spirit there and told the ghost to speak up. One person said that they heard a ghost say the word, "Anger."

Did that mean that someone in the basement was angry? Why? Were they mad because of the visitors or because of something that happened long ago? Was this ghostly spirit the one who many had seen moving the Tommyknocker's eyes?

As the ghost hunt ended, the television crew packed up to leave. They were careful as they headed up the stairs, cautious not to bump the Tommyknocker and make the spirit angrier. No one wanted to get a look from those creepy eyes . . .

Now that the store is permanently closed, we have to wonder, just where is that Tommyknocker?!

CHAPTER 10

The Washoe Seeress

You've already read the story of Eilley Bowers, who went from being wealthy beyond imagination to telling fortunes for the locals in Virginia City. Her knowledge of the future, and the prophecies she told through her peep stone (crystal ball), became legendary. Even after losing her own fortune, people trusted her visions. Eilley's fortune-telling became her business and she was known as the "Washoe Seeress."

One young man came to see her after he'd been robbed. He sat with Eilley and told her that a bag of valuable gold dust was missing. She consulted the stone, and the spirit world, then did what the police had be unable to do. Eilley solved the crime. Not only did she tell him who had the gold dust, but she told him exactly where to find it.

The man rushed from Eilley's parlor, straight into Six Mile Canyon. There he found the crook and his bag of gold dust. After regaining his treasure, he returned to town to share his good news. After that, people came to Eilley to solve their mysteries.

One of her cases involved

a missing ring. The stone was valuable, but it also held great sentimental meaning. Eilley peered into her peep stone and let the owner know that the ring would be returned within a week.

"Stop searching," she said. "There is nothing to do but wait."

A week later, the ring was found! Eilley was more popular than ever.

She helped the local milliner, Mrs. Hickox, find a missing insurance policy. Mrs. Hickox had lost a large envelope of important papers. Having exhausted every other way to find the documents, Mrs. Hickox went to see Eilley. She was desperate.

Eilley told the woman that the papers had been stolen. She described the thief. Mrs. Hickox recognized the person as one of her customers! And when she thought about it further, she realized that the customer had been in the shop the same day the papers went missing.

Mrs. Hickox went to see the customer and sure enough, she found the missing papers! The customer apologized and promised to make things right. As for Mrs. Hickox, she went to the newspaper with the story. She knew it seemed strange that a fortune-teller helped her, so she declared that if anyone doubted the truth of the story, that she'd be willing to swear under oath that Eilley's powers were real.

Eilley's skills grew stronger and in time, she not only could read the future, but she also could communicate with the dead. In 1878, she received a message from a man named Joe who had died years earlier. He told her that his grave was unmarked and that his spirit couldn't rest. Could she help him?

The spirit directed her to Cemetery Hill. Eilley went to find the grave. From there, the problem was easily solved. Eilley asked the caretaker to show her the place where he'd buried Joe.

A few minutes later, she stood in front of a plot. Eilley placed flowers on the grave. Joe was no longer forgotten. It's said that his spirit was grateful and spread the news of what she'd done for him. Now, other ghosts in the cemetery were also convinced of her abilities and they felt they could come to her with requests too.

As she got older, Eilley moved from Virginia City to Reno. She opened a small fortune-telling and séance business there. She communicated with a man named Joseph Rover. He'd been accused of murdering his business partner. The ghost assured Eilley that he hadn't done it!

Eilley believed Mr. Rover. She tried desperately to convince the authorities that

Mr. Rover was innocent. She said that his spirit needed peace and the only way was for the police to find the actual killer. The people she talked to made fun of Eilley and didn't believe her. But twenty years later, a man made a shocking confession on his deathbed. He revealed that he had actually been the one to kill Joseph Rover's business partner. Mr. Rover was innocent after all.

Eilley Bower's died penniless and alone in 1903. She'd given up fortune-telling and had moved to Oakland, California. The new owners of the Bower Mansion in Virginia City brought her ashes back to town so she could be properly buried near her family. And her spirit is said to roam the mansion grounds.

There is the unmistakable clink of champagne glasses, reminiscent of the lavish life and wonderful parties she and Sandy once held. Eilley lives on in the space where she had a lovely house, fine gowns, expensive art from England, and riches to spare.

She has chosen to haunt the best part of her life. Wouldn't you?

CHAPTER 11

Ghost Wagon

When you're looking for ghosts in Virginia City, you're sure to come across a few surprises. One night, ghost hunters were out along D Street, hoping to see something special. And they did!

As they walked along in the moonlight, they were snapping photos, searching for the glowing orbs that would let them know ghosts were nearby. They also had an EVP recorder, a machine that would let them record and play back ghostly sounds and voices.

It was late, the streets were deserted, and the town was completely silent. Suddenly, the quiet was shattered by the clatter of horse hooves and coach wheels barreling down the street. The ghost hunters jumped to the sidewalk, out of the way, but there was nothing there. No wagon. No horses. The street was empty.

The next day, they learned that this ghostly wagon has traveled up and down D Street for

years. Many people have witnessed it. If you were on D Street late one night and heard a wagon approach, would you be afraid? Or would you try to hitch a ride?

Main Street, Virginia City

CHAPTER 12

On the Hunt

The ghost wagon on D Street didn't frighten the ghost hunters, and they were determined to find more ghosts. Just past the church, they had another sighting. One person saw the spirit first, then everyone caught a glimpse. Some didn't think it was truly a ghost because the way the figure stood seemed far too real.

They called out, "Hello!"

The person took a step back as the group moved forward.

Was someone else out this late at night? Were they looking for ghosts too?

No. In a flash of movement, the figure melted away, disappearing right before the ghost hunters' eyes. It seemed to drop into the ground and melt away.

Not looking for ghosts—it was a ghost!

D Street was once a busy part of Virginia city, so it's quite possible that there could now be a lot of ghosts wandering along the street or haunting the local shops.

A ghost is known to haunt the Gold Strike gift shop building. Two shoppers went into a small area at the back of the store that was set up for a fortune-teller.

"Look at that old woman," the man told his girlfriend. He pointed at an empty space in the room.

The girlfriend didn't see anything.

"Over there," the man insisted. "She's looking right at us."

She still didn't see anything. "Must be a ghost," she joked.

"You need your eyes checked," her boyfriend said.

His girlfriend stared at the spot. Was it possible there really was someone there?

After leaving the shop, the spirit of the old lady followed them out.

The boyfriend suddenly shrieked. "Did you see that? That old lady just ran up and bopped me on the nose!"

The woman looked at her boyfriend. Sure enough, there was a small bump on his nose that was bleeding Now, she had no doubt that he was telling the truth. It hadn't been a joke at all. There had been a ghost in the shop and for some reason, it followed them into the street!

Seeing ghostly spirits is common around town, but seeing ghost pets happens less frequently. Still, some claim that they've witnessed Ruffles, a fox terrier, wandering around.

Ruffles was owned by a man named Earl and his wife, Ida. The couple had owned several dogs over the years, but Ruffles was their favorite. Earl and Ruffles were inseparable. When Earl died of a heart attack, the dog passed shortly after. Ida didn't get another dog.

A few years later, a couple moved into a home directly behind her house, and Ida decided to introduce herself over the fence.

The neighbors asked how she kept her garden so lovely. "Doesn't your dog destroy the flower beds?" they asked.

"What dog?" Ida asked.

"The little dog that wanders into your backyard sometimes. I've seen a man come to the fence and call him to come outta there a couple times," the woman said.

Ida was confused. She checked the fence for holes, but then didn't think any more about the dog that her neighbors had seen.

One rainy, cold afternoon, when Ida was watching TV, the neighbor woman who had seen the dog came by. She'd locked herself out of the house and needed a place to wait until her husband came home. Ida welcomed the woman inside. The woman came in and looked around the room. When she spotted a photo of Earl and Ruffles on the fireplace mantle, she

smiled. "Why, that's them, the little dog and the man I've seen in your backyard."

Ida smiled. "You're mistaken, dear," she said. "That's my husband and his dog. They've been dead five years."

The woman gasped and said, "I've seen them as clearly as I see you!"

At least Earl and Ruffles were still together in the afterlife—and mindful of Ida's flower beds.

CHAPTER 13

The Clock

If you work at the Virginia City Visitor's Center, you work side-by-side with a ghost. No one knows for sure who it is, but she was there first. This playful spirit is believed to be either a former owner of the building or a favorite customer from the days when the building was a bar.

Whoever it is, she's having fun. The ceiling chandelier flickers off and on at random times. Papers get rearranged on desks. Pencils disappear. There are cold breezes on warm days. The smell of coffee and smoke linger in empty spaces.

Usually, those who work in the building just laugh when the ghost does something silly. If you can't find your notes for the big meeting, or you go to get your pen and discover that it's not where you left it, well, those things are funny. But sometimes, on rare occasions, the ghost gets mad.

Workers at the Visitor's Center know that it's better not to disturb the ghost if it's in the storeroom. For some reason, that is private space and no one wants to hear a disemboweled voice shout "Get out!" It's happened so many times that it's best to avoid the area if you think the ghost is around.

The strangest thing about the Visitor Center ghost surrounds the Crystal Bar's old clock. The clock hands move on their own to random times during the day. Maybe the ghost is trying to pass on a message from beyond.

If you think you can figure out what the ghost is trying to say, hurry to the Visitor's Center. Those who work in the building would love to know . . .

CHAPTER 14

The Most Haunted Hotel

Miners that swarmed to Virginia City hoping to get in on the silver rush needed a place to stay. That's why the Gold Hill Hotel was built in 1861. So many different ghosts haunt this hotel that you have a good chance of bumping into one there.

Rosie and William are the most well-known ghosts that hang around. Employees say they are usually friendly and never get in the way.

Most people believe that William is the spirit of a man who once owned the hotel. But who is Rosie?

One rumor is that she was an elegant lady who was killed in a carriage accident. The incident was near the hotel, so it was natural that her spirit would go to the most lavish spot nearby. And from the very beginning, this hotel was very lavish. It was beautiful, with expensive furniture, polished wood, and elegant fabrics. A lovely lady who liked the fine life might want to stay in a place like this after her death. Another story says that she was not a wealthy lady in life, so she is finally living her dreams now in death.

Guests and employees say it's the scents of these spirits that come first. William smells of cigars. Rosie gives off the odor of fine perfume. They have been known to "appear" at lectures in common spaces and in hotels rooms as well.

A woman who was staying in Room 5 at the hotel heard her daughter-in-law wandering in the hallway, just outside her room, late at night. Every time she fell asleep, her daughter-in-law would start stomping down the hall. The woman knew her daughter-in-law was interested in ghosts and thought that maybe she was trying to get a photo of Rosie and William. But, wow, could she do it without making so much noise?! It was hard to sleep.

In the morning, the woman confronted her daughter-in-law. She was mad, but also curious. She asked, "Did you get any good photographs?"

The daughter-in-law stared at her. "What do you mean?"

She said, "I heard you in the hall last night. You weren't being very quiet about it."

"Wasn't me," she said. "I slept like a log last night."

They both realized that it must have been one of the hotel's ghosts making noise in the hall! But, was it Rosie? Or maybe it was William?

William behaves as if he is overseeing the hotel workers. Staff often report feeling a cool gust of air, seeing a shadow in a corner, or smelling a cigar when they are busy working. Sometimes, they even work harder when William is around, as if the boss has come to check up.

If you don't find Rosie and William at the hotel, maybe the cowboy ghost will be there. Ghost hunters think this is the spirit of Jabez Spencer. He was murdered in front of the building in 1871. It's common for people who had traumatic deaths to stay near where the event happened, so it seems clear that the most obvious identity for the cowboy ghost would be Jabez.

Jabez was a nice, simple man, who worked as an engineer for the mills in the valley. He married a young woman, but they didn't get along well. People reported seeing them argue all the time. Some say that James Murray fell in love with Jabez's wife.

One evening, James and Jabez ran into each other on the street in front of the hotel. After a short argument, they each drew a pistol. James was the quicker shot, and he shot Jabez in a jealous fit. Jabez died instantly.

A hundred years later, a photographer was standing outside the hotel, taking pictures of the beautiful sunset. He was surprised to find a ghostly cowboy in his photos. The photographer hadn't noticed anyone standing there while he was snapping pictures. The ghost only appeared in the pictures when they were printed. Professional ghost hunters were called to examine the photos. The ghost hunters all agreed. There was no way they were fake! Was this the ghost of Jabez Spencer? Maybe . . .

Come to the Gold Hill Hotel and check it out for yourself. William, Rosie, and Jabez are waiting for you.

The Silver Queen

CHAPTER 15

The Silver Queen

The Silver Queen Hotel is a favorite spot for ghost hunters. You'll often find investigators with their hunting and recording equipment lingering in the hallways trying to make contact with spirits.

The best place to start any ghost hunting tour of the hotel is at the famous painting. The Silver Dollar Lady is an image of a woman in a dress. The dress takes up an entire wall and is made of 3,261 silver dollars. Tourists come from all around the world to look at the painting and take selfies with it. In addition to her silver dollar dress, the Silver Dollar Lady is wearing a belt made from twenty-eight twenty-dollar gold pieces.

The painting isn't very old. It was made in the 1950s. Jeri Eaton, the former hotel owner had the painting commissioned. She also was the model for the painting.

One night, Jeri Eaton was shot at the hotel. Her death was called an accident. It was determined that Jeri was cleaning her own gun and shot herself. But was that the truth? Was there more to the story?

Just a few months later, Jeri's husband, Carroll Walter Eaton, married Ruby, a teller at the bank. Immediately after the wedding, Ruby began to make changes to erase Jeri from the hotel's history. Everyone knew that Jeri Eaton had posed for the Silver Dollar Lady. But now, the gift shop postcards were changed to say that it was Ruby in the artwork.

A medium, a person who can communicate with the departed, arranged a séance at the hotel. The medium immediately made contact with Jeri. The ghost had a lot to say. Jeri told those at the séance that she was not angry. She simply wanted people to remember her. The people at the séance promised to tell her story and she seemed satisfied with the answer. Jeri's ghost is not gone from the Silver Queen, but when she does show up, she seems proud to be there and happy to be remembered.

Another ghost at the Silver Queen is a man named Tiny Carlson. Tiny also owned the hotel for a while. Two hotel guests shared that they were checking out of the hotel and told the clerk how wonderful their stay was in Virginia

City. They shared that there was a very nice hotel employee in the hallway.

"He told us all about the history of the hotel and even offered us a cookie." they said.

"There's no one working up there," the clerk assured them.

"Yes, there is," the insisted. "He's a short, old man carrying a tin of cookies."

Right away, the clerk realized that the guests had met the ghost of Tiny in the hallway. Tiny had diabetes, and couldn't enjoy sweet treats, but in death, he often had a tin of cookies.

The guests were surprised. Maybe they should have taken a cookie. What did ghost cookies taste like?

Some of the rooms at the Silver Queen are also haunted. If you stay in Room 13, be prepared to hear a ghostly couple arguing late in the night. They've been shouting at each other for over a hundred years. Room 11 has a spirit that cries at night. Another room has a ghost that plays tricks, moving your stuff around.

Then, there's the elderly ghost that sits outside sometimes. Some say this ghost is Florence Ballou Edwards. She owned the hotel in 1945 and spent thousands of dollars upgrading it. Those who see her say she's easy to recognize. Florence was short and a little round. She often has her ghost dog with her.

In addition to Jeri, Tiny, Florence, the arguing couple, and the ghosts in Rooms 11 and 13, the ghosts of a little boy and a teenage girl have also been spotted. Some people say that they've have heard a baby mysteriously crying somewhere in the building as well. There are so many ghosts around that if you find yourself staying at the Silver Queen, you may want to make check that anyone you see in the hallway is actually alive . . .

Mackay Mansion

CHAPTER 16

Where to Search

We've talked about a lot of ghosts in Virginia City so far. Would you believe there are more? When you are in town, there are hot spots where ghost hunters like to search for spirits. If you haven't encountered ghosts already on the street or at your hotel, maybe try these other places.

Two ghostly nuns haunt the St. Mary's Art Center, which used to be a hospital. The White

Nun is more well-known than her ghostly companion. The White Nun often stares out of the building's third-story window late at night. Her story is that fate sealed her doom one night long ago when a terrible fire broke out in the hospital. She died in the blaze, but saved many lives that night. Now she stands watch over the place, still protecting the people inside.

At Piper's Opera House, the ghost of the founder John Piper is said to linger. He's often there for the opening of a new show. John enjoyed a cigar, so if you smell smoke, it's likely he's around. He's the only one allowed to smoke in the otherwise "no smoking" building.

Other sightings in the opera house include ladies and gentlemen who are still enjoying the shows, long after they passed on. Phantom actors and actresses share the stage with the living. And several years ago, a rude ghost was said to be pinching people as they entered the theater.

If you didn't find the spirits you were looking for in the theater or the Art Center, try Mackay Mansion. There is a ghost there that is reported to show up every afternoon at exactly 3:00. He's rarely late.

At the Chollar Mansion near the Chollar Mineshaft, there is a ghostly gentleman dressed in fine clothing. He walks up and down the mansion's stairs. There are forty steps so that's a lot of exercise, even for a ghost. He enjoys reading books from the bookcase and keeps mostly to himself. If you see him, be quiet. He likes his solitude.

Buy some fudge at Grandma's Fudge shop and say hi to the ghosts that haunt the backroom. They are pranksters and will topple pans or scare customers by suddenly laughing out loud.

Up and down the streets of Virginia City, wherever you are . . . beware of ghosts.

Conclusion

It seems that every building in Virginia City has ghosts! It's an old town, so that's not surprising. Ghost hunters have come from around the world to meet and greet, to learn about who haunts the city. Television shows have been recorded in town. But you don't have to have to be a professional ghost hunter to see spirits. You don't need any special equipment to find haunted spaces in Virginia City. Just keep your eyes open. Listen for unusual sounds. Breathe deep and check for unfamiliar scents.

Virginia City is one of the most haunted places in the United States. Don't be afraid. Most of the spirits will welcome you. Only a few will try to scare you away.

Come and meet them for yourself.

I dare you.

New York Times Best Selling author **Stacia Deutsch** has written more than three hundred children's books including The Jessie Files, a spin-off of the beloved Boxcar Children mystery series. Stacia lives in Temecula, California, where she is a member of the historical society and loves hearing spooky stories! Find her at www.staciadeutsch.com. Instagram @staciadeutsch_writes and www.facebook/staciadeutsch.

Check out some of the other Spooky America titles available now!

Spooky America was adapted from the creeptastic Haunted America series for adults. Haunted America explores historical haunts in cities and regions across America. Each book chronicles both the widely known and less-familiar history behind local ghosts and other unexplained mysteries. Here's more from *Haunted Virginia City* author Janice Oberding: